BOW HUNTING BASICS FOR BEGINNERS

BOB POPE

© Copyright 2003 Bob Pope. All rights reserved.

No part of this publication may be reproduced, stored in a retrieval system, or transmitted, in any form or by any means, electronic, mechanical, photocopying, recording, or otherwise, without the written prior permission of the author.

National Library of Canada Cataloguing in Publication Data

Pope, Bob, date-
    Bow hunting basics for beginners / written by Bob Pope.

ISBN 1-4120-0356-3

    1. Bowhunting. I. Title. II. Title: Bowhunting basics for beginners.

SK36.P66 2003   799.2'028'5   C2003-902706-6

TRAFFORD

This book was published *on-demand* in cooperation with Trafford Publishing.
On-demand publishing is a unique process and service of making a book available for retail sale to the public taking advantage of on-demand manufacturing and Internet marketing. **On-demand publishing** includes promotions, retail sales, manufacturing, order fulfilment, accounting and collecting royalties on behalf of the author.

Suite 6E, 2333 Government St., Victoria, B.C. V8T 4P4, CANADA
Phone   250-383-6864   Toll-free   1-888-232-4444 (Canada & US)
Fax   250-383-6804   E-mail   sales@trafford.com
Web site   www.trafford.com   TRAFFORD PUBLISHING IS A DIVISION OF TRAFFORD HOLDINGS LTD.
Trafford Catalogue #03-0725   www.trafford.com/robots/03-0725.html

10   9   8   7   6   5   4   3   2

BOW HUNTING BASICS FOR BEGINNERS

BOB POPE

TABLE OF CONTENTS

Acknowledgments 5

Introduction 7

Chapters

1. BOW AND ARROWS 9

2. BOW ACCESSORIES 17

3. NO SEE ME-NO SMELL ME 33

4. TREE STAND OR GROUND BLIND .. 49

5. SHOOTING YOUR BOW 71

6. WHERE TO HUNT 83

7. PUTTING IT ALL TOGETHER 95

ACKNOWLEDGMENTS

A special thanks to my wife, Judy, and daughter, Stacy, who put up with all the days I was gone hunting thru the last 25 years.

Thank you to my friend and author, Steve Wood. Your encouragement inspired me to make the move and write my first book.

Thank you to my brother-in-law, Larry, for sharing his hunting tips and thoughts with me on most of my hunting trips. I couldn't have asked for a better hunting partner.

Thank you to Trafford publishing for all of their professionalism and help in making it possible to see a dream come true.

ABOUT THE AUTHOR

Bob Pope is a hunter, author and speaker who has spent more than 35 years hunting whitetails with 25 of those years devoted to bow hunting.

Most of his hunting experience has come from hunting in the northern counties of Michigan in big woods habitat on state and federal land.

His vast knowledge of hunting skills makes him very qualified to teach others the basics to become a successful bow hunter.

Contact Bob at:

Email : hunterbobp@wideopenwest.com
Web : www.hunterbob.com

INTRODUCTION

If you have the desire to bow hunt, commit yourself to be the best bow hunter you can be. You owe it to yourself and to the game you hunt.

 Some 25 years ago I decided to try my hand at bow hunting. The moment I drew my first arrow back, I was bow struck! Over the next several years, I learned by trial and error what worked and what did not. I turned some hard learned lessons into some well deserved success stories.

 The intention of this book is to help you get started in bow hunting. I've tried to occupy the pages of this book with basics to get you pointed in the right direction. Fancy words and high tech terms have been left out. In their place, just plain and simple information designed to help you become a successful bow hunter.

Subjects like how to select the right bow, arrows, accessories, hunting from a tree versus staying on the ground, advice on the proper hunting clothes and staying scent free. This and much more to prepare you for that moment when you must make the first shot and harvest your first deer. Good Hunting !

CHAPTER 1

BOW AND ARROWS

The first time you walk into a bow department you may be overwhelmed by how many different bows there are to choose from. The bow manufactures today all make quality bows in a wide range of prices. You don't have to pay top dollar any more to get a quality bow that will perform well for you. However, any old bow will not do. This is your most important hunting tool and it must not be taken lightly. Go to a local archery pro shop that has an archery range as well as a knowledgeable archery staff or pro. Bass Pro Shop and Cabelas are just two of the outdoor sports stores that fit this bill. I have had many good experiences with both of these fine establishments. They will answer all of your questions and will help fit a bow to your personal needs and wants.

WHAT KIND OF BOW

Your pro will help you choose between a traditional bow and a compound bow. He will show you the differences in each one and then the decision will be left up to you. The majority of bow hunters today use a compound bow. Again, this is a personal matter of choice. Take the time to test fire a number of bows, paying close attention to the comfort of the bow in your hand and how quiet the bow is upon release of your arrow.

DRAW LENGTH AND DRAW WEIGHT

Part of the bow selection is determining your draw length and draw weight. Draw length is simply the distance from the bowstring, when pulled fully back, to the back of the bow handle. Many beginner bow hunters make the common mistake of choosing a bow with a draw length that is too long for them. Your pro will determine your correct draw length for you.

Draw weight is simply the amount of force needed to pull your bow back to its maximum draw length. Be sure to choose a draw weight that you can comfortably handle. Do not choose a draw weight that you have to strain to pull back. You should be able to put your bow out in front of you and draw the string straight back. If you start pointing the bow toward the sky in order to get it pulled back, the draw weight is too heavy for you. This will only result in loss of bow control causing you to shoot inaccurately. Again, listen to your pro and his recommendations.

CHOOSING YOUR ARROWS

When you have finally made your bow selection, you will also need help in choosing the right arrow shaft.
Most hunters today use either aluminum, carbon, or a combination of both materials for their arrows. Carbon arrows are becoming very popular as of late but the aluminum arrow is still used by the majority of hunters today. Before you make your decision on which kind of arrow to use, have your pro show you the differences in each one. He will then help you choose the right shaft based on your draw weight.

FLETCHINGS

Once you have decided on an arrow shaft, you must also decide on a choice of arrow fletching. Fletching is simply the material found on the nock end of your arrow. The nock is the part of the arrow that holds the shaft on the bowstring. The fletchings job is to keep your arrow flying straight. There are two basic fletching materials. They are plastic vanes and feathers. You will hear hunters swear by both but the most popular vane used today is the plastic vane. Probably the biggest reason is that temperature and weather have little effect on the plastic vane. This is not the case however with feathers. Water is its worst enemy. In my hunting experiences, plastic vanes have worked the best for me. They hold up in all kinds of weather conditions.

In the next chapter we will talk about all the accessories that can be added to your bow to help make you a more accurate shooter. We also will talk about paper tuning your bow. This is a very important step in assuring that you have proper arrow flight.

NOTES

NOTES

NOTES

CHAPTER 2

BOW ACCESSORIES

Now that you have made your bow and arrow selection, we will take a look at a few of the many accessories that are available to you to improve your accuracy in shooting.

ARROW RESTS

Few archery accessories have improved more in the last 10 years as the arrow rest has. Fewer still have more sizes, styles, and designs, making it a very confusing decision on which one to choose.

You will need a rest that is quiet, as the arrow glides across it, and also one that allows the fletchings to pass thru the rest unobstructed.

One type that fits the bill is the prong type rest. This rest has been the choice of most hunters today due to the fact that it works well with releases and a majority of bow hunters use some type of release aid. We will talk more about mechanical release aids later on in this chapter. The prong type rest is worth taking a close look at as your choice of rests.

One rest I have found success within the last few years is the fall away or drop away rest. It is a prong style rest that upon release of your arrow, falls out of the way and allows no contact with your arrow fletchings. Arrow fletchings have a definite effect on arrow flight if they come in contact with the prongs of your rest and the fall away rest eliminates any chance of this happening.

Ask your pro to let you test fire an arrow using the fall away rest before you make your final selection in an arrow rest.

MECHANICAL RELEASES

Another decision you will have to make is whether to release your bow string with your fingers or with a mechanical release aid. We will examine the basic differences in each.

If you are going to use fingers to release your bow string, you will need finger tabs to protect your fingers. Without protection for you fingers, you would develop rawhide like skin, or calluses, or both. For these reasons alone, the majority of bow hunters today use some type of mechanical release aid to release their bow string. A release aid will also produce a more accurate arrow flight than finger tabs for the simple reason that you are attaching your release to one point on your string, making your release consistent every time. With finger tabs you have to worry about releasing all three fingers from the bow string smoothly at one time, a tough order to follow.

   Lets look at the mechanics of a release aid. A release aid is made up of a strap, which goes around the wrist, a base, which is attached to the strap, and a trigger and jaw which are part of the base. When you strap the release around your wrist, the base with the trigger and jaw fit in your hand like a pistol. The jaw is attached to your bowstring. After you have pulled your bow string back, the trigger is pulled to provide the release of your bow string.

There are a multitude of styles and designs of releases to choose from. Ask your pro to allow you to test fire some arrows using a mechanical release. This will allow you to get the feel of the release and help make your decision on what stye you might choose. A word of caution. Don't go cheap. While most manufactures today make quality releases, they will cost you some bucks. In this case you get what you pay for and cheap is not the way to go.

PAPER TUNING

The basics are now in place on your bow to do a paper tune. Paper tuning, simply put, is an arrow shot thru a piece of paper which is set in front of a regular target. After the shot, the tear in the paper is examined. Different types of tears indicate different types of arrow flight.

Your ultimate goal is to achieve a bullet hole tear in the paper. Your pro archer will determine what adjustments need to be made to achieve this. You are now ready for a bow sight.

BOW SIGHTS

There are two accessories that you will want to have in connection with your bowsight. They are a peepsight and a kisser button. We will look at these two important accessories later on in the chapter but right now let's look briefly at the basic bowsights offered on the market today.

Fixed pin, moveable pin, crosshair and pendulum are the most used bow sights today. Before I go any further on this subject, I would like to recommend that you buy the best bowsight your budget will allow. If you skimp here, you are headed for some major disappointment. The best bow and arrows will not make up for a cheap sight. When you put your sight pins on a target, you want to know that where you are aiming is where your arrow is going to strike. Some lesser quality sights do not hold their aim through many shots. This is not good! The really good pro archery shops will allow you to test fire your bow with a sight of your choice so you can see if your sight is holding its aim. Take full advantage of this whenever possible. Now let's take a look at the sights available to you today.

FIXED PIN SIGHTS

The fixed pin sight is the most popular sight on the market today. The fixed pin sight provides one or more pins set for precise distances. Though not as precise, other distances are sighted between the pins. These pins are attached to a sight bracket which surrounds the pins and guards against the pins being knocked out of tune. The sight bracket is attached to your bow handle.

CROSSHAIR SIGHTS

Cross hair sights provide a bow shooter with a vertical and horizontal reference point by means of wires connected to a sight bracket. They are very accurate. The horizontal wire is moveable, up or down, to give you sights at various distances.

MOVEABLE PIN SIGHTS

The moveable pin sight has the advantage of being able to adjust your pin to the target distance. The disadvantage here is when your target appears suddenly and there is no time to adjust, you end up guessing where to aim.

PENDULUM SIGHTS

These sights were produced mainly for those hunters wanting to hunt from tree stands. It's designed with one pin that pivots on a hinge. The tree stand hunter, high in a tree, aims right on his target without making any adjustments and the pin pivots to the precise spot he is aiming at. One disadvantage with this sight is because of the moveable parts, they can be a bit more noisy than other sights. Most hunters I know that use these sights swear by them. Check them out.

PEEP SIGHTS

A peep sight is simply a small see thru

aperture that is inserted between the strands of your bowstring. When you draw back your bow string, you line up your sight pin in the center of your peep hole and then aim onto the spot you want to hit on your target. The peep sight will definitely make you a more accurate shooter. The peep sight will need to be installed by your pro. He will have you draw back your bow string to full draw and then mark your string where the peep sight should be installed. This is one accessory you don't want to be without.

KISSER BUTTON

A kisser button is simply that, a button. It is installed on your bow string and used as an anchor point. An anchor point is the point at which your bow string is pulled back to full draw and you keep it at that point all through your aim until release.

Many bow hunters use the corner of the lips(kisser) as their anchor point. The button, installed in your string, is drawn to the corner of the lips(anchor point) and that is how it became to be called the kisser button

BROADHEADS

Broadheads are simply the razor sharp blades, on the end of your arrow, that are used to harvest an animal. The choices available to you will seem unlimited. Don't be afraid to ask your archery shop pro for some guidance when making your selection. We will take a look at the most used types of broadheads today.

FIXED HEAD BROADHEADS

A fixed head broadhead is two, three, or four non replaceable fixed blades attached to a center ferrule. A ferrule is the part of the broadhead that secures the blades in place. The ferrule is then screwed or glued to your arrow shaft. This type of broadhead is most popular with hunters using longbows, a straight one piece bow. The disadvantage with this broadhead is that the blades are not replaceable. They must be resharpened by the archer and the entire broadhead replaced when the blades wear out.

REPLACEABLE BLADE BROADHEADS

The most popular kind of broadhead used by hunters today is the replaceable blade broadhead. When the blades become dull, they can be easily replaced with new blades. This is done by simply inserting the new blades into the ferrule and then screwing the ferrule into the end of the arrow causing the blade ends to become locked into place. They are an excellent choice for hunting.

MECHANICAL HEAD BROADHEADS

The mechanical head broadhead has started to be used more and more in the last few years. It's big advantage over the other two types of blades discussed here is arrow flight.

The other broadhead blades are held in a fixed open position, extending out from the ferrule. As the blades hit the air, they tend to steer the arrow off course. With the mechanical heads, this is eliminated. This is because the blades of the mechanical head are partially folded back into the ferrule before the shot, eliminating air flow on the blades. At impact on the target, the blades open up wide and lock in place to expose the cutting edges just like the other broadheads. This enables a bowhunter to target practice with practice points and not have to worry about there being any change in arrow flight when changing to broadheads. My personal experience with these blades has been limited to the practice range only and they work very well.

Be sure to ask your pro to let you test these broadheads before making your final selection. They may be the right broadhead for you.

 In the next chapter we will look at a couple of very important subjects. Staying out of sight and staying scent free.

NOTES

NOTES

CHAPTER 3

NO SEE ME- NO SMELL ME

We will now talk about two very important subjects. Staying out of sight and staying as scent free as possible.

In all my hunting years, the two most common mistakes I have seen hunters make are:

    1.) Not taking the proper steps to eliminate as much of their scent as possible.

    2.) Sticking out like a sore thumb in their hunting area.

In this chapter we will look at some things you can do to overcome both of these mistakes.

STAYING SCENT FREE

Entire books have been written on how to defeat a deers sense of smell but the most that can be hoped for is to create a little confusion with his nose. You will never become totally scent free but there are steps you can take that will help you cover or eliminate most of your scent. Let's look at a few of them.

PERSONAL HYGIENE

One of the easiest things to do is to keep yourself as odor free as possible by washing your body with a scent free odor eliminating soap. There are a number of different brands on the market today that do an excellent job at attacking bacteria before it can emit body odor and being odorless at the same time. If you are going to be hunting for 3 or 4 days or longer and a shower is not going to be available, there are even disposable scent free, odor killing wash cloths that work very well. Just make sure after taking the time and effort to wash with scent free products that you don't go somewhere, like a restaurant, and expose yourself to all kinds of domestic scents that will for sure defeat all your good intentions of being scent free. I can't tell you how many times I have seen hunters come out of an eating establishment, dressed to hunt , and go directly to the woods and wonder why they didn't see a deer all day. Don't be caught making this fatal mistake.

COVER SCENTS

You will also find scent free deodorant that works well and a multitude of cover scents that claim to cover up your human scent. Make sure you use some common sense when choosing cover scents. For an example, skunk scent will definitely cover any human scent but when does a skunk give off this awful odor ? When there is danger and a deer recognizes this too ! This may not be your best choice.

SPRAY COVER SCENTS

A couple of spray cover scents I've had a good deal of success with are Scent Shield fall blend and Scent-a-away human scent neutralizer. The fall blend smells like the woods in the fall after the leaves start falling and is a scent that the deer are very comfortable with. The human scent Neutralizer smells like nothing, which is good! The cover scents are sprayed directly on your hunting clothes or boots and neutralize any odors that might be detectable by a deers nose.

A couple of other good scents happen to come in a round plastic wafer form. They are fresh earth cover scent and white oak acorn scent. The fresh earth scent smells like a handful of dirt and the white oak acorn scent smells like freshly fallen white acorns. You keep them stored in a round plastic container when you are not using them and like magic their odor reactivates just like they were new. I use them in my bow case, my backpack and my boot storage box.

DRYER SHEETS

   Another great product that came out a few years back is dryer sheets that are scented in fresh earth scent. They work just like the fabric softener dryer sheets that your wife uses to make your clothes soft and static free. Just throw them in the dryer with your hunting clothes and the heat works with the sheets to make your clothes come out smelling like dirt.
   My wife often complains when I'm using these scented sheets as the odor flows out the dryer vent to the outdoors. One day when I was drying my hunting clothes she happened to be outside near the dryer vent and she said, something smells just like dirt! I knew then that the sheets were doing their job and they do work very well on giving your hunting clothes the smell of fresh earth. What could be more natural to a deers nose.

SCENT FREE LAUNDRY DETERGENT

The next thing you want to pay attention to is what you wash your hunting clothes in. This means everything right down to your underwear and socks. Wash them in a scent free detergent and dry them outdoors the old-fashioned way on a clothes line or in the dryer using the scented sheets mentioned earlier in this chapter.

SCENT FREE STORAGE

After you have your clothes washed and scent free, you will want to store them in an air tight storage container or bag so they don't pick up any scent between the time they are washed and the time you start your hunt.

Many hunters use clear plastic bags for their storage and these work very well. Just recently I came upon a product that has produced excellent results in airtight storage and also saving space. It is simply called The Bag.

It's an airtight, economical clear plastic bag with a zipper at one end of the bag and a one way air valve at the other end. You place your clothes in the bag, zip it closed and then roll the clothes toward the one way air valve. All of the air in the bag is forced out the other end of the bag thru the one way air valves. After compressing the items in the bag you can store them rolled, flat or folded in less than half the space then they were before. The best thing is the items in the bag are totally airtight, making it impossible for any foreign odors to penetrate.

You get three bags, one extra large bag and two large bags for under twenty bucks. That's a great deal and I highly recommend that you give them a try.

   The best thing I have found for storing your boots is a storage box with hinged lids or snap covers. I place a couple of earth scent wafers in the box with my boots and when I am ready to put them on they smell just like fresh dirt.
   The bags, storage boxes and scent wafers can all be purchased at your favorite outdoor hunting store.

SCENT FREE CLOTHES

   A major break through in hunting clothes came on the scene several years back. It is charcoal liners that you wear like long underwear underneath your outer hunting clothes. These liners absorb any body odor and keep it locked within.

The most recent development to come on the market is hunting clothes with activated charcoal incorporated into the fabric lining of the cloth. This has made the need for liners obsolete. However many hunters continue to use them because of the considerably higher cost of the carbon lined clothes.

There are several quality manufactures of carbon lined clothes. My experience has been with the Scent Lok brand. My hunting success has really changed for the better since I have changed exclusively to wearing these carbon lined clothes. I've watched deer walk to my stand on the very path I took and sniff every twig and plant that I may have touched and not become alarmed. I attribute this to the

Scent Lok clothes I was wearing. This same scene when I was not wearing carbon lined clothes, resulted in the deer catching my scent and high tailing it into the next county leaving me frustrated and wondering what happened.

As you can see, these clothes do make a difference in helping you keep your scent contained. If you practice good hygiene with scent free products, wash your clothes in scent free detergent, store them in air tight storage containers and use carbon lined clothes, your chances of seeing more deer will increase significantly.

I've had some hunters tell me that this is too much trouble to do all this. They are the same hunters who complain to me that they're just not seeing as many deer anymore or that the deer always seem to be just out of their range to shoot. Wake up fellow hunters !! THEY SMELL YOU ! Take the time to take the necessary steps and become as scent free as possible. You will see more deer and become a more successful hunter. I did !

INVISIBLE IN THE WOODS

I believe that playing the wind (in your face), being scent free, and wearing the right patterns and colors of camouflage clothing will help you get close to a deer and an opportunity of a lifetime.

QUOTE: THE ONLY THING WE CAN'T BRING CLOSER IS OPENING DAY !

Camouflage clothing will not make you completely invisible but almost. It will sure help you blend in to your hunting surroundings enough that deer will not recognize that you are there. Most of the deer that I have harvested have only been ten to twenty yards away from my stand. To be that close and not be detected is a sign of an experienced hunter. It is my intention to try and save you a lot of frustration by giving you some basics, along with some tried and proven lessons, to become a <u>experienced beginner</u> in the art of staying hidden in the woods.

  The first thing I look for in camo clothing is if the fabric is quiet. If your clothing makes noise as you draw your bow back, it won't matter what color or pattern your camo is, your busted !! The unnatural sound of a fabric with a scratchy surface, in close range of a deer, will send that deer in to the next county. I always check camo that I might buy by scratching its surface with my fingernail and if it makes any noise, it stays on the hanger.

The second thing I look for is the color that will match the hunting area I will be in. For example, you wouldn't wear leafy brown camo if your hunting in pine trees but rather light and dark greens. Save the leafy browns for hunting in the fall before the leaves start falling and are still in full color.

The last thing I consider is patterns. I try and stay away from solid patterns and lean towards patterns that offer contrast in their shapes to help break up my outline. Trebark, Advantage and Realtree are just a few of the camo patterns on the market today and all of them work very well. There is even a leafy 3-D pattern (mentioned earlier) offered for early fall. They are a bit pricey but very realistic and my choice for early fall hunting. All of the camo manufactures offer many colors to help you reach the level of concealment you'll need for your hunting country.

A suggestion that has worked very well for me is to take a picture of the area of the woods, at the time of the year you plan to hunt, and then take that picture with you to your favorite hunting store and match it up with the patterns and colors most closely resembling your area. Your archery pro will be able to help you with this decision.

In the next chapter we will look at different types of tree stands and ground blinds and the safety you need to practice while using them.

NOTES

CHAPTER 4

TREE STAND OR GROUND BLIND

WHY USE A STAND

One of the most effective methods of hunting deer today is with some kind of stand. Why are they so successful? Most offer a lot of concealment, such as ground blinds, or they are elevated high enough above the animals line of sight that they normally don't see you. There are two basic types of stands, tree stands and ground blinds. Let's look at each one.

TREE STANDS

Tree stands are the most common and popular stands used by bow hunters today. Two good reasons are deer don't always look up and elevation helps in keeping animals from catching your scent. There are many different kinds of tree stands on the market today. Let's look at a few.

CLIMBING STANDS

Climbing stands were one of the first portable tree stands to come on the bow hunting market. They are usually in two pieces with both being attached around the trunk of the tree with a blade or rope that bites into the bark as you apply pressure to it. You stand on the lower half while raising the upper half with your arms and securing it in place. You then lift the lower half up with your legs while sitting on the upper part and then repeat the whole process making your way up the tree.

This is the bottom part of the climbing stand. Notice the blade at the top part of this climbing stand. There are wing nuts on each side of the blade that you can detach which allows you to fit the blade around the trunk of the tree and then back on to the climbing frame. This blade digs into the tree when you apply pressure to the stand which you do by standing up . Notice also the straps that are attached to the bottom of the stand. These are for your boots to slip into allowing you to lift the stand with your legs.

This is the top part of a climbing stand. Notice the seat towards the bottom of the picture. The large blade on this part of the stand detaches the same way as the bottom, with wing nuts.

Usually there is a safety cord securing the upper part of the stand to the lower part in case the lower part of the stand were to slip off your boots. The safety cord keeps this from happening.

This type of stand works very well as long as you have a tree with no limbs to interfere with the climb. Early on in my bow hunting adventures I used this type of tree stand with a lot of success. I still have my original climbing stand and still put it to use from time to time when the conditions call for it.

FIXED POSITION STANDS

Fixed position stands are the most popular stands today. Unlike the climber, it must be hung on the tree in a fixed position. It is also called hang on stand.

Hang on stands have a seat and a platform that are attached to a metal frame. The frame is attached to the trees trunk with a strap or a chain. I like the type that uses a rachet strap to secure the stand to the tree.

It is quieter than a chain and provides a rock solid attachment. Many manufactures provide a T-screw as part of the hang on stand. A T-screw is simply a bolt like screw with a T on one end. The screw is threaded part way into the tree with the T part protruding out away from the trunk.

A special bracket built into the stands frame fits over the T and holds the stand in place until the rachet strap can be placed around the tree securing the stand in place.

The T-screw is then screwed the rest of the way into the tree securing the frame tightly against the tree. Final adjustments of the ratchet strap are then made to make sure that the stand is locked tight against the tree and will not move once you step into it. Make very sure that you are wearing a safety belt or harness while tending to all of these procedures in placing your stand.

CLIMBING STICKS

In order to hang your tree stand you will need a way to get up the tree. Screw in steps used to be the most popular method in making your way up the tree but many states have outlawed them because they do damage to the trees. Strap on or tie on tree steps have taken the place of the screw in type. Although these work fairly well, I have found that climbing sticks work better for me.

They are easy to put together and light enough to carry over your shoulder thru the woods to your selected stand sight.

You can spray paint them with camo paint to match the bark of the tree and they are very reasonably priced.

Notice the ratchet strap securing the climbing stick to the tree.

Climbing sticks come in three or four foot sections and they are made so that they slide together to form a long pole with alternating steps on each side of the pole.
The sections can be put together all at one time and then put up next to the tree

or you can attach one section to the tree and then slide the next section into the first, secure it and go on to the next section. I prefer to do all sections at one time and then put it up next to the tree. This allows me to see if the ladder will fit straight up without coming in contact with any limbs.

The sections are attached to the tree with tie on straps or ratchet straps. Again, I have found that ratchet straps work best for me because of the stability

they provide. Ropes work very well but do not always remain tight like the ratchet straps. Most manufactures today provide ropes with their climbing sticks. If you want ratchet straps you must provide them yourself at an extra cost.
Always remember to wear a safety belt or harness when installing climbing sticks to a tree. Don't take a chance and become a victim of a fall while preparing for what you love to do. It's not worth it. Be safe!

LADDER STANDS

This type of stand is simply a ladder with a seat and a foot platform built at the top of the ladder. They are very easy to climb and very easy to install but are not portable. Their bulkiness and weight do not make it practical for moving them around whenever you feel like it. Almost all of them require a helping hand when setting them in place. Also the ladder is by no means hid from anyone or anything(deer).

These type of stands are used primarily on private land where they can be left up all year round after they have been placed.

SAFETY AND TREE STANDS

Safety should be the first thing on a hunters mind when climbing to a stand, while in his stand and when descending from his stand. A safety belt must always be used in each of these situations. It may seem like a lot of trouble but not near as much trouble if you should take a fall. When installing climbing sticks for steps, a safety belt allows you the freedom of using both hands to get your installation done easily and quickly. If you're not using one, one hand has to be on the tree at all times while you try and install something with the other. This is not a safe situation.

Another thing to keep in mind is never ascend or descend your stand carrying your bow or anything else in your hand. You need both hands to climb. Attach a rope to your stand that reaches to the ground. When arriving at your stand, attach your bow to the rope and after climbing to and into your stand, pull your bow up. Reverse the process before leaving your stand.

I have recently changed to a safety harness, which is put on much the way you put on a shirt. The harness goes over both shoulders and back and around me in the front, snapping together like a belt. The safety belt part is attached around the tree and has a loop that attaches to the middle of my harness in the middle of the back. If I were to fall I would be kept in an upright position and hopefully in a better position to get myself back into my stand. Be safe! Stay safe!

NATURAL GROUND BLINDS

Simply stated a ground blind is a stand built on the ground. Although many more deer are taken from tree stands than from the ground, ground blinds do have their place in bow hunting. There are some very good advantages to hunting from a ground blind. Number one is you can't fall out of a ground blind! They also can be made very comfortable and you can almost totally conceal yourself with the help of natural downed branches etc. If you have the right natural material such as pine or cedar around your stand, you may be able to help cover your scent.

  Ground blinds definitely have a place in bow hunting so don't think of them in only terms of rifle hunters. I have shot many fine deer from ground blinds using my bow and I don't hesitate for one minute to build one if the situation calls for it.

  Recently I have come across some hunting area that is loaded with deer sign. A tree stand is out of the question because there are no mature trees to handle a big tree stand. Do I forget about this place? No way !! This summer I will be building a ground blind in a predetermined spot found on a scouting trip this past winter.

  There have been times that I should have been spending all day in the woods hunting but the thought of being in a tree for that length of time kept me from following thru. Shame on me ! I should have built a ground blind for that occasion.

For those hunters who do not like heights or simply cannot climb a tree, ground blinds become your only choice. Ground blinds can be an advantage and should not be ruled out if the situation calls for it. Think out of the box! You'll be surprised what will come to you.

PORTABLE GROUND BLINDS

Portable ground blinds have become very popular in the last few years. The main reason for this is that they are portable. I know a lot of impatient hunters who find it very difficult to sit in one place for very long, especially if they are not seeing any action. They are prime candidates for portable blinds.

Most manufactures of portable ground blinds have made them light and easy to assemble. Some manufactures claim you can put them up in less than a minute. They have spring loaded frame work, much like an umbrella and they pop right open. Some even claim to trap your scent inside the blind much like Scent Loc clothes. You don't even have to open a window to shoot. The window openings are covered with a mesh that you can actually shoot an arrow thru without it effecting arrow flight. While these high tech blinds are costly, they do seem to work very well. If you don't like the spot you are hunting, you pack up the blind and move very easily to another spot. What could be easier.

Take a close look at these blinds. They do work in the bow hunters bag of tactics.

NOTES

NOTES

NOTES

CHAPTER 5

SHOOTING YOUR BOW

Learning all of the things you need to do to consistently make good shots is not an easy task, but it can be done. Others have done it before you and you can do it too. We will look at several things I think are essential to making a good shot. Once you master these you will be on your way to becoming a good archer. You owe it to yourself and to the game you pursue.

STANCE

Stance is a very important part of your shot. Place you feet far enough apart to maintain good balance, usually twelve to eighteen inches apart.

Use an open stance which is a position that pivots your chest toward the target. This moves your bowstring away from your chest and bow arm ensuring clean string travel and a accurate shot.

DRAWING YOU BOW

To draw your bow, hold it out in the direction of the target and draw the string back smoothly to your anchor point. Once you get the string drawn back to its anchor point, it's time to take aim.

TAKING AIM

Aiming and holding is easier with a compound bow because of the letoff factor found in all compound bows.

The best way to explain letoff is by an example.
If you have a sixty pound pull with a sixty five percent letoff it means you are holding forty pounds less than sixty, or twenty pounds at full draw. When you feel that snap at full draw, your compound bow has just let off sixty five percent of your draw weight making it much easier to hold your bow string until you have taken aim.

Aiming is really a simple process if you are using a peep sight and sight pins. You simply line up the correct sight pin in the center of the peep sight and then on to the spot on the target that you want to hit. Hold it there until your steady and then release. From the time you draw until the time you release should be no longer than six to seven seconds. That probably seems like a very short time but as you become an experienced archer that is all the time you will need under hunting conditions.

There will be times when there will be exceptions to this rule but you will amaze yourself how automatic this will become as you improve day by day.

RELEASE

  A smooth release is of the utmost importance to accurate shooting. Squeezing the trigger of a mechanical release and not jerking it will lead to consistently good shots. Try not to anticipate the release of your arrow. As you squeeze your trigger on the release, the release should be a complete surprise to you and this will keep you from jerking your shot. Only through much practice will you develop the skills needed to produce a smooth release shot after shot.

A common mistake by many hunters is they leave practicing to just before the opener of hunting season. Practice is what makes you a better shot and it must be a year around commitment if you really want to become an expert. Once or twice a week is good during the off season to keep the muscles loose. As the hunting opener draws close, step up your practice time to three and four times a week to really polish your skills. Remember: Practice makes Perfect

FOLLOW THRU

Follow thru is just as important as a clean crisp release. Keep the bow arm perfectly still, but relaxed as the arrow is released. A common mistake by beginners is in their excitement they drop their bow to see where the arrow hit. This results in the arrow going off line. Your goal is to continue aiming at the target until your arrow actually hits. This will probably be one of the toughest things to overcome as you learn to become a good shot. You will have to practice this over and over before it will become second nature. However, once you have got this down, you will notice your accuracy improving tremendously.

<u>YOU SHOOTING RANGE</u>

When the time comes to take your shot, stay within your shooting abilities. If your target is not within your shooting range, don't take the shot. As you practice you will come to know what yardage you are comfortable shooting at and what yardage your are the most accurate at. This is your shooting range.

Most experienced bow hunters harvest a deer from less than thirty yards. I rarely take any shot over thirty yards because I'm most comfortable and very accurate at this range. As a beginner I would concentrate on shots twenty yards and under. When you have enough practice at this range and feel confident you can put an arrow within a six inch circle on every shot, then you are ready to move out to targets a little farther away. Don't let your ego get in the way of your brain. You will only be disappointed and may end up injuring an animal rather than becoming successful. You owe it to yourself and to the game we pursue to stay within your confident shooting range.

   Another thing to keep in mind is to always be aware of the deers body language. Is he walking stiff and alert ? Is he stomping his feet ? This means that he is not real comfortable with something and this is not the right time to take a shot. He is on red alert if you notice these body signals and a shot now no matter how close he is could result in the deer beating your arrow.

Believe me when I say that deer have split second reflexes and at the sound of a bow string being released, they can and have jumped out of the way of a launched arrow. This is called jumping the string. Wait until a deer is in a relaxed state if you can before you take a shot. Signs of this are when a deer is browsing thru the woods nibbling on leaves and buds of trees, looking up slowly and wagging his tail.

These body signals tell me that a deer is in a relaxed state and this is when you want to make that shot. You still have to be quiet and wait for the right moment when the deer is not looking your way, but your chances of him jumping the string go way down when they are relaxed rather than nervous.

PRACTICE MAKES PERFECT

It is very important that you start practicing well before the season opener. Don't limit your practice to just shooting at a target with a bulls eye. If your budget will allow you, purchase a life size deer decoy so you can practice shooting at something that is close to the real thing. Most decoys will outline the vitals of the deer on the body so you will know where to aim.

If your going to be hunting from a tree stand, be sure and set up your stand in a tree at the same height you will be hunting from and practice some shots at your decoy. This will prepare you for the real thing and also show the angle of entry of your arrow from high in a tree. Sometimes you have to make some adjustments on your point of aim into the deer because of the angle of the shot. You may be hitting your spot on the deer but because of the angle of entry, the arrow may be missing the vital area as it comes out the other side of your target. This is a very important detail that many tree stand hunters don't pay attention to and then wonder why their shot didn't do the job.

Another very good practice tool is to attend some 3-D archery hunts at your local hunting club. Many clubs put on these shoots during the summer and they are open to the public for a small entrance fee to their range.

This is real good practice as they are usually in a wooded setting and the decoys are usually set up differently at each station. You travel around to each station and estimate the yardage and then take your shot. Some shots are from the ground and some are from platforms off the ground. Some shots are from inside a blind and some are from sitting positions. It is a real change of pace for all hunters to go thru instead of just shooting at home in your backyard.

Try one out this summer. You'll enjoy it and it is very good practice.

NOTES

CHAPTER 6

WHERE TO HUNT

A whole book could be written on this subject alone. In this chapter I will give you some basics on where to hunt. I will not cover everything but I will cover some key elements I think are crucial in stand placement. They are scouting, wind direction, feeding areas and bedding areas.

SCOUTING

To understand the big picture of the area you are going to hunt you must do some serious scouting for main deer trails going between bedding areas and feeding areas.

If properly done, pre season scouting is the key to successful stand sites.

Pre season scouting is very simply a matter of recognizing where the favorite food sources are and finding the travel routes between the deers bedding area and the food source. Find these two important areas and you are on your way to an opportunity to harvest a deer.

I have had a great deal of success scouting in the months directly following the end of deer season. In my state of Michigan, this is in January and February. Although the weather can be pretty nasty during these months, it is the best time to pinpoint feeding areas, bedding areas and major runways. The travel routes used in the winter are very similar to those used in the fall and they show up very clear in the snow covered woods. Many times if you follow these you will jump deer from their beds and you have discovered one piece of the puzzle. Once you have located the bedding area the food source will not be far away. Now you can decide where to locate your stand somewhere in between these two areas. Try not to get to close to the bedding area and also set up somewhere off the runway, not right on it.

In early fall I look for a good food source such as white oak stands. White oaks produce the sweetest acorns in the woods and the deer favor them over black oaks. Be sure to learn the difference between the two oaks so you can readily spot them in the woods. Once I've located a runway leading to the oak stand, I start looking for a stand site adjacent to the runway and in my bow range of the oak trees. I also make sure that I can get to and from my stand without the deer hearing or seeing me. Pay close attention to this. If you can't get to your stand without alerting the deer of your presence, look for another site that will allow you to do so. If you scout early and often, I am confident that you will find a good place to intercept deer and place a stand. It won't matter if your in a ground blind or in a tree, you will be where the deer are going to be and that is more than half the battle come opening day!

DEER MOVEMENT

There are three times of the day when deer move the most. They are dawn, mid morning to mid afternoon and dusk. Most hunters hunt the dawn and dusk hours. This is usually 6 a.m. to 9 a.m. and 4 p.m. to 7 p.m. If you are going to hunt the morning hours it is best if you arrive at your stand site at least an hour before light. This gives the woods time to settle down before it becomes legal to shoot.

Once you get to your stand, get settled quickly and quietly and then remain as still as possible. Become part of the woods and everything around you will be unaware that you are even there.

If your hunting in the evening, arrive as early as you like but remain on stand until after dark and then walk out. Many fine deer have been harvested at last light.

In the last few years I have added the midday hours for hunting to my battle plan. Contrary to what a lot of hunters believe, deer do move during the hours of 10 a.m. and 2 p.m. including trophy bucks! When every other bow hunter is leaving the woods after an early morning hunt, pack a lunch and spend 4 hours, from mid morning to mid afternoon, hunting from your favorite stand. You may be pleasantly surprised at how many and what kind of deer show up in your area. Why is this? After as little as 2 times walking to and from your hunting stand at the same time each day, deer have patterned you. They will wait until you have left at your usual time and then enter the area knowing you are gone. Change your time and see more deer. Don't get patterned!

STAND PLACEMENT

Hunting animals on their own turf is not an easy task. You are invading their living room and if you are not careful in how and where you set up your stand, you'll be busted before you even hunt your stand for the first time.

Let's think out side of the box for just a few paragraphs. Think about your own living room at home. Everyday you come home from work and go into your house and your living room and look for your favorite easy chair so you can kick back and relax for a while. You know where everything is in relation to that easy chair. The end table next to your chair where you keep the remote for the t.v., the lamp that sits on the other side of your chair, the picture on the wall above the couch. You get what I mean?

If you were to come home one day and your table that holds your remote was gone, or your lamp table on the other side of your chair was gone, would you notice it? Of course you would! It's no different with the deer. If they come home one day to their living room and see a great big clump of newly cut branches in the middle of their house, do you think that it would go unnoticed?

How about that big blob up in their favorite oak tree that they eat acorns at all day? What's the point?

When placing your ground blind or tree stand in a deers living room, use some common sense. Keep things looking as natural as you can and don't make big changes to the immediate area.

Build a ground blind around a tree that has already fallen and just add enough like natural material to give yourself some cover. You want to blend into the woods and look like you are part of it, not something that stands out.

If a tree stand is what you use, try and find 2 trees side by side and position your stand between them so you look like part of the trees.

One trick I have used with a great deal of success is to find a tree that is dead or dying that still might have some cover at it's top and put it up against my stand for some natural cover. Because the tree is from the area it doesn't look out of place and it helps me blend in to the surroundings.

Have more than one stand. If you have done your scouting you more than likely have come upon more than one good area. Limiting yourself to just one stand will cause you to over hunt the area and may lead to the deer finding you out. I make it a practice to hunt a stand no more than 2 days in a row and at different times .This assures me that the deer are not patterning me and it also gives me a change of scenery.

LOCATION ! LOCATION !

The best way to determine where to locate your stands is thru scouting. I have already mentioned this before but it is so important that it warrants saying it again. SCOUT !!

Scouting will help you determine where the feeding locations are going to be the best come autumn.

To become a little more precise I will discuss an area of the woods that I have had a lot of success with. That area is called the "EDGE". An edge is where 2 or more habitat types come together. As an example, where a stand of oak trees butts up to a pine stand , the boundary where they meet is the edge. Another example is a clear cut meeting a mature forest.

Many times our forestry will cut down 40 acre plots in the middle of the woods to promote new growth. This cut is known as a clear cut. Within that same year, new growth will start to appear and deer can be found browsing on this new growth.

Deer relate to edges and seem to feel secure around them. Finding an edge is a great place to put your first stand and will provide you with a good opportunity to harvest a deer as long as some of the other elements are in place, such as food source, and travel routes. Take advantage of the "EDGE".

NOTES

CHAPTER 7

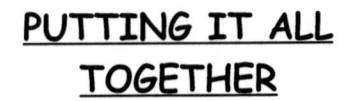

PUTTING IT ALL TOGETHER

"WHERE ONCE STOOD A BEGINNER, NOW STANDS A HUNTER"

My formula for success is summed up in the following equation:

"Preparation"+"Focus"+"Positive Thinking" + "Patience"= SUCCESS!

I believe that there is no such thing as luck in hunting deer. Oh sure we all have heard about the first time hunter walking into the woods and sitting down on the first comfortable stump he came to and shooting a big buck 15 minutes later. Is this luck? I'm not sure but it has been said that when luck occurs, it is when an opportunity meets preparation.

I believe this with all my heart. Things just don't happen in the bow hunters world. You have to do your homework before success comes your way. Try and take a shortcut or rely on luck and you will be a unhappy hunter.

When you are out there against the elusive whitetail, make sure you have prepared yourself to be the best bow hunter you can be. When on stand, focus all of your attention on seeing deer. Stay alert !

Be positive. Believe in yourself and your abilities. Your thoughts should be> I know I'm going to see deer and I will be successful.

Be patient ! Be persistent and stay that extra half hour even though you haven't seen any deer all morning. So many times early on in my bow hunting experiences I gave up and on my way down the tree I would see a deer standing 60 yards off from my tree watching me climb down. If only I had waited just a few minutes more. A hard lesson but I learned from it.

Learn to think "just beyond the obvious". Try to think like a deer. Why is he using this runway and where is he going.

Remember, food is what causes deer to move most of the time. For bucks, when the does come into their time, this is what causes them to move and make mistakes. Place yourself where you can intercept these movements and you will harvest your first deer.

The more I learn about the whitetail, the more I am amazed and the better I understand how they so easily evade us hunters.

FINAL THOUGHT

Upon the harvesting of a deer, I have always felt an inner sadness with respect to ending a life. A life filled with more freedom than I will ever know. I have always taken a quiet moment to pay my respects to such a majestic animal and to thank my creator for the freedom I have that allows me the privilege to spend time in the woods. Good Hunting!

NOTES

NOTES

NOTES

NOTES

NOTES

BOW HUNTING BASICS FOR BEGINNERS

Subjects to help the beginner get started in bow hunting. This book is filled with bow hunting subjects and strategies to help the beginner become knowledgeable in bow hunting technics. This book will help prepare you for your 1st hunt or your 50th hunt.

Author Bob Pope shows you how to:
* Select a bow
* Pick bow accessories
* Decide on what type of stand
* Stay scent free
* Aim your bow
* Stay safe while hunting from heights
* Scout

An easy to read book that uses simple terms and explanations to ensure you understand what it takes to hunt whitetails successfully.